FOURTH OF JULY

Manchester-By-The-Sea, Massachusetts

Written and Illustrated by Alice Gardner

To the people of Manchester-By-The-Sea.
Thank you for your friendliness, help, and
wonderful love of your beautiful town.

Copyright © 2021 by Gardner Publishing,
Beverly, Massachusetts

ISBN 978-0-578-64571-1

DO YOU KNOW WHAT A TRADITION IS?

It is something special people or a community enjoy doing year after year, usually at the same time and the same place.

The tradition of holding a Fourth of July parade and festivities in Manchester-By-The-Sea dates back many, many years. The oldest reference to a Fourth of July parade, found in the archives at the Manchester Historical Museum, is July 4, 1829! Incorporated in 1645, the town of Manchester-By-The-Sea celebrated its 375th anniversary in 2020.

America's birthday, the Fourth of July, has been celebrated in many different ways over the past 192 years in Manchester-By-The-Sea.

1898

Children had a decorated bicycle parade at 8 a.m. Prizes for winners were a bicycle bugle, a searchlight lantern, a Christy saddle, a bicycle bell, and a bicycle pump.

At 10 a.m. there was a 100-yard dash, a three-legged race, a potato race, a swimming race, a pole-walking contest, and an aquatic-horse contest. Prizes ranged from one to three dollars, and there was a special prize for the most comical costume.

At 2 p.m. a Fireman's Parade was held.

From 4–6 p.m. was a concert by the Hutchings Military Band, followed by fireworks at 8:30 p.m.

TODAY

A red, white, and blue pancake breakfast is held the Saturday before the Fourth of July at Tuck's Point.

A concert and fireworks are held at Singing Beach on the night before the Fourth of July every even year, and a concert is held at Masconomo Park every odd year.

At 10 a.m. the parade begins!

After that you will be thrilled to watch the sky divers at the local elementary-school field jump from a plane, unfurl their colorful parachutes, and land right on the designated "x" spot!

HAPPY FOURTH OF JULY TO MANCHESTER-BY-THE-SEA, MASSACHUSETTS!

American Flag

Antique Cars

B

Balloons

Bag Pipers

Boy Scouts

Concert

Declaration of Independence
Drums
Dixieland Band

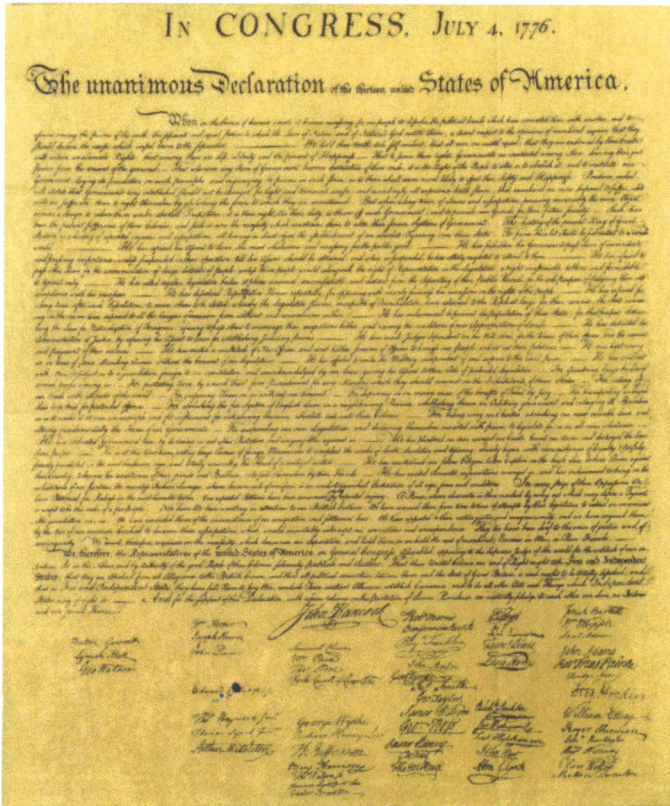

We hold these truths to be self-evident, that all men are created equal, that they are endowed by their Creator with certain unalienable rights, that among those are Life, Liberty and the Pursuit of Happiness.

E

Elephant

F

Forster Flag

Flag Cake

Fire Engine

Games

100 Yard Dash | 3 Legged Race | Potato Race

Hot Dogs

Hamburgers

Happy Birthday America

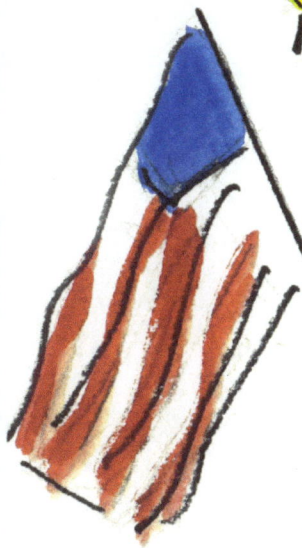

Ice Cream

July 4th

JULY

Sun	Mon	Tues	Wed	Thus	Fri	Sat
1	2	3	4	5	6	7
8	9	10	11	12	13	14
15	16	17	18	19	20	21
22	23	24	25	26	27	28
29	30	31				

K

Kilroy's
Jambalaya
Jazz Band

Little League
Champions

M

Mexican
Mariachi
Band

N

Necklaces for July 4th

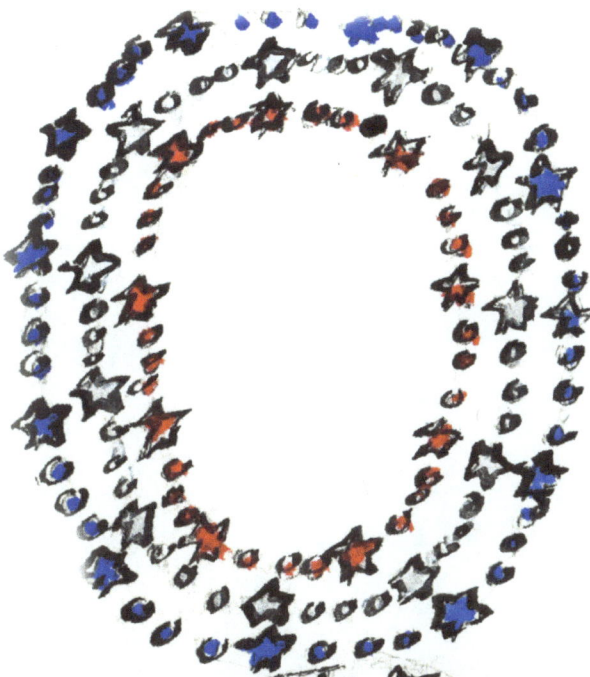

Ocean

Penny Farthing Bikes

Queue

Red White and Blue

Pancake Breakfast

Second Massachusetts
Regiment Softball

MANCHEST
ESSEX
Softball

Tenth Massachusetts Regiment

Uncle Sam

Volume II

Steel Drum Band

Veterans

LET FREEDOM RING

W

Whale

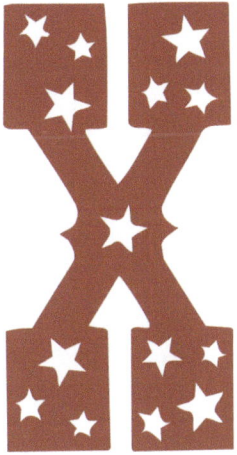

X Marks the Spot

Yankee Doodle

YANKEE DOODLE

FOLK SONG

Yan-kee Doo-dle went to town, a - rid-ing on a pon - y. Stuck a feath-er in his cap and called it "Mac-a-ron - i". Yan-kee Doo-dle keep it up, Yan-kee Doo-dle Dan - dy. Mind the mu - sic and the step and with the girls be han - dy.

bethsnotes.com

Zany

Big Smile
ENTERTAINMENT

Do you know these fun facts about the Fourth of July?

American Flag

On June 14, 1777, our first official flag was approved by the Continental Congress. It had 13 stars on a blue background and 13 red and white stripes, both representing the 13 original colonies: Virginia, New York, New Hampshire, Massachusetts, Maryland, Connecticut, Rhode Island, Delaware, North Carolina, South Carolina, New Jersey, Pennsylvania, and Georgia. As our country grew, more stars were added to the flag but the original stripes remained the same. In early 1959, Alaska became the 49th state and Hawaii's star was added later that year to make 50 stars. Today we celebrate the birth of the stars and stripes on June 14th—Flag Day!

Antique Cars

Everyone looks forward to seeing the antique cars in the annual Fourth of July parade in Manchester-By-The-Sea. A line of over thirty-five amazing cars lead off the parade. You can see cars like a 1929 Ford woodie, a 1930 Chevy, a 1929 Packard touring car, a 1937 Ford convertible, a TR3 convertible, a 1954 MGTS, a 1966 Cadillac, a 1969 Mercedes Benz 280SL, and a 1971 Citroen.

Concert

A concert with fireworks is held every even year at Singing Beach in Manchester-By-The-Sea. A concert at Masconomo Park on the harbor is held every odd year. Singing Beach was named for the singing sound you hear as you shuffle your feet in the sand. It is one of very few beaches on the North Atlantic Coast with sand that "sings." Sand sings when it is round and between 0.1 and 0.5 millimeters wide, contains silica, and is at a certain humidity. The best part of the beach to hear singing sand is on the dry side, above the normal high-tide lines.

Declaration of Independence

The Declaration of Independence was written to inform the British Parliament and King George III that all 13 colonies under British rule were declaring their independence. It was approved by Congress on July 4, 1776. Copies were printed and delivered to all 13 colonies where it was read in public and printed in the newspaper. A copy, of course, was sent to King George. Liberty bells rang out and America was born. We now celebrate America's birthday every year on the Fourth of July.

Forster Flag

Nearly 250 years ago, the Minutemen of the Manchester Company of the Essex County Militia responded to the Lexington alarm and took off for Lexington. 700 British redcoats were advancing on Concord and were planning to destroy a cache of military supplies. The Battles of Lexington and Concord were the first battles in the American Revolutionary War, both fought on April 19, 1775.

The Manchester Company carried the Forster Flag. The flag was named after Samuel Forster, a Manchester ship master who was a second lieutenant. Each regiment needed a flag so the soldiers could find their group if they became separated. It is believed that 2,000 flags may have flown in the American Revolution. Each regimental flag was unique, most picturing regional symbols like pine trees and beavers. The Forster Flag was the first flag with 13 white stripes to represent the thirteen original colonies. The flag was about five feet long, crimson in color, with six stripes in the left-hand corner on one side and seven stripes on the other.

The Forster Flag remained with the Forster family in Manchester for the next 200 years until it was sold to the Flag Heritage Foundation in 1975. The Forster Flag is believed to be the oldest surviving flag from the American Revolution.

A reproduction of the Forster Flag can be seen at the Manchester Historical Museum. The flag is flown every year in the annual Fourth of July parade in Manchester-By-The-Sea and is carried by the Tenth Massachusetts Regiment.

Ice Cream

Captain Dusty's, on Beach Street on the way to Singing Beach, is a very popular ice cream shop in Manchester-By-The-Sea.

Back in 1946, Bruce Leseine, who was later known as Captain Dusty, opened a fish and lobster shack at that location. His wife Margaret worked at the counter and Bruce did the fishing and lobstering. For most of the six decades they lived in Manchester, they were the only black residents.

Captain Dusty was known for his generosity, sense of humor, and good will. When interviewed later in life, he said, "This town has taught me something: It is not the color of your skin or the size of your wallet that makes a good man." He died in 1990 at the age of 85.

July 4th

Every year since 1776, the United States of America celebrates its freedom from Great Britain's rule on the Fourth of July.

On July 2, 1776, the Continental Congress voted in favor of independence; two days later, delegates from the 13 colonies adopted the Declaration of Independence.

John Adams wrote to his wife Abigail that Independence Day "will be celebrated, by succeeding Generations, as the great anniversary Festival . . . with Pomp and Parade, with Shews, Games, Sports, Guns, Bells, Bonfires and Illuminations from one End of this Continent to the other."

In the early days during the Revolutionary War, families put lighted candles in their windows to celebrate and show support of the ongoing war. Since that time, the Fourth of July is celebrated with family gatherings, picnics, parades, concerts, and fireworks.

In 1781, Massachusetts was the first state to make the Fourth of July an official state holiday. In 1941, it became a federal holiday.

P

Penny-Farthing Bikes

One of the highlights every year of the old-fashioned, Manchester-By-The-Sea Fourth of July parade is watching the riders on the Penny-farthing bikes. They sit high on the bikes and seem to handle them with ease, even as they sit very high above ground.

The Penny-farthing bike, also known as the "high wheel," "high wheeler," and "ordinary," has a large front wheel like the English penny, and a much smaller wheel like the English coin called the farthing. The farthing coin is worth one quarter of a penny. These coins were used in the mid 1880s. The Penny-farthing was the first machine to be called a bicycle. Frenchman Eugene Meyer designed the first high wheeler in 1879 and is considered the father of the high wheeler; it was a spoke-tension wheel with individually adjusted spokes. Englishman James Starley added the tangent spokes and mounting steps to his famous bike called the "Ariel." Starley is considered the father of the British cycling industry.

The Penny-farthing bikes could go very fast and were considered to be quite dangerous. Manchester-By-The-Sea's *Cricket* explains why it's dangerous in the "Burroughs to Pedal History": "The problem with high wheelers is learning how to ride them without 'taking a header' or a fall. The trick is to hop on the step on the backbone or frame, increase forward motion to stabilize the bike, re-establish your own stability on the bike, and then get onto the seat and maintain your balance."

In the late 1880s, James Starley's nephew invented the Rover Safety Bike with the seat located much closer to the ground. The Penny-farthing bike began to lose its popularity. The pneumatic tire was invented by John Dunlop and wheels on bikes were smaller and safer.

Many people still love the elegant design of the antique Penny-farthing bikes. Many antique versions are ridden in parades and festivals to the delight of onlookers. Joff Summerfield set off in 2006 for a two-year journey around the world on a Penny-farthing. Tasmania, Australia, is host to the National Penny Farthing Championships every year.

R

Red, White, and Blue Pancake Breakfast

The Red, White, and Blue Pancake Breakfast takes place every year at the Chowder House at Tuck's Point. The event is held on the Saturday before Fourth of July. You will see two other well-known structures on Tuck's Point Road: the Manchester Yacht Club and the Rotunda. All three structures were built in the late 19th century.

Tuck's Point was named after Captain William Tuck, a very successful privateer—a person who privately owns an armed ship. His ship was authorized by the government for use in the Revolutionary War, especially to capture enemy merchant ships.

Captain Tuck is best known for the day he and his crew were captured by a British frigate. An elite crew of British officers took over his ship, the Buccaneer, and sailed it to Halifax, Nova Scotia, Canada. Captain Tuck apparently liked to socialize and got along well with the British officers. Upon reaching Halifax, he was invited to join the British officers for dinner on the mainland. In the meantime, his first mate, Daniel Leach, and his shipmates decided to take matters into their own hands. While the British were working on some rigging, Daniel Leach and his shipmates took an axe and smashed into a chest of guns. The British sailors did not have time to grab their own guns and were taken prisoner. When Captain Tuck arrived back at his ship with the British officers, Daniel Leach informed the British officers that they are now prisoners and Captain Tuck was able to captain his ship and sail to Boston.

When Captain Tuck died in 1826 at the age of 86, the town decided to celebrate his successful career and named the harbor near his home "Tuck's Point."

Uncle Sam

Samuel Wilson and his brother Ebenezer owned a meat-packing business in Troy, New York. Samuel had served in the American Revolution at age 15 and was known for his honesty, fairness, and service to his country. He was well liked in the community and many people called him "Uncle Sam."

During the War of 1812, meat was in short supply for the soldiers. Secretary of War William Eustis contracted with Elbert Anderson, Jr., of New York City to distribute meat to all soldiers in New York and New Jersey for a year. Samuel and his brother won the contract to supply Anderson with the meat. They were required by the government to stamp the packages of food with "EA.-US."—contractor Elbert Anderson (EA) and the United States (US). Many of the soldiers were originally from Troy and knew Uncle Sam and his meat-packing company. When the soldiers saw "US" on the packages, they decided it stood for Uncle Sam who was helping to feed the army.

A local newspaper picked up the story about Uncle Sam feeding the soldiers. His name began to be associated with the American government; over time, Uncle Sam became a popular nickname for the American government and the symbol of what you can do for your country.

Wilson was born in Arlington, Massachusetts, and died on July 14, 1854 at the age of 87. You can visit a memorial in Arlington, as well a memorial in Riverside Park in Troy, New York—the self-proclaimed home of Uncle Sam. You can also visit Wilson's childhood home in Mason, New York.

The artist James Montgomery Flagg (1877–1960) created the most famous image of Uncle Sam with a tall top hat, blue jacket, and red-striped pants. The image was used in World War II to encourage young men to enlist in the military. Uncle Sam was pointing his finger in the image and saying, "We want you!"

In September 1961, US Congress recognized Samuel Wilson as "the progenitor of America's national symbol of Uncle Sam."

Yankee Doodle

The song "Yankee Doodle" was originally sung by the British soldiers who made fun of the American soldiers during the Revolutionary War. The British called the soldiers from the East Coast "Yankees" for being so inexperienced and disorganized. As the Americans began to win the war, the American soldiers started to sing "Yankee Doodle" and took it over as their own. They created many new verses.

Yankee Doodle went to town
A-riding on a pony.
Stuck a feather in his cap
And called it macaroni.

Chorus:

Yankee Doodle keep it up,
Yankee Doodle dandy,
Mind the music and the step,
And with the girls be handy.

The word macaroni was used in Great Britain to refer to the outlandish fashions the aristocratic men brought back from their tours of mainland Europe in the 1760s. The outfits consisted of gigantic wigs, tight-fitting clothing, striped stockings, and colorful shoes. To be a macaroni was to be in style. A "doodle" to the British was a simpleton or a person lacking common sense. When the British sang, "stuck a feather in his cap and called it macaroni," they were saying that the American soldiers naively thought they could stick a feather in their hats and be as fashionable as a British macaroni.

In 1781, with the surrender of the British at Yorktown, "Yankee Doodle" became a song of national pride in America. In 1978, "Yankee Doodle" was adopted as the state song of Connecticut.

References

American Flag

Memling, Carl. *Our Flag*. New York: Golden Book, 2011.

"The History of the American Flag—For Kids." Americanflags.com. June 27, 2016. americanflags.com/blog/post/history-american-flag-kids.

"History of the American Flag: Lesson for Kids." Study.com. March 21, 2016. study.com/academy/lesson/history-of-the-american-flag-lesson-for-kids.html.

Concert

"Singing Beach at Manchester-By-The-Sea." Atlasobscura.com. atlasobscura.com/places/singing-beach-at-manchester-by-the-sea.

Forster Flag

Parker, Susan. "Forster Leach Family Lecture" (lecture). Manchester Historical Museum, Manchester-By-The-Sea, Massachusetts. April 22, 2017.

"The Forster Flag: Endowing a Legacy." Briscoe Center for American History. cah.utexas.edu/news/press_release.php?press= forster_flag.

Herwick, Edgar B. III. "239 Years Ago, Minutemen Flew The Forster Flag, The First with 13 Stripes." WGBH. April 18, 2014. wgbh.org/news/post/239-years-ago-minutemen-flew-forster-flag-first-13-stripes.

"The Historic Forster Flag." Doyle Auctions. April 9, 2014. doyle.com/auctions/14ff01-forster-flag/historic-forster-flag.

Ice Cream

Huss, John. "What's In A Name?" (lecture). Manchester Historical Society Annual Meeting, Manchester-By-The-Sea, Massachusetts. June 5, 2018. manchesterhistoricalmuseum.org/whats-in-a-name.

July 4th

Dalglish, Alice. *The 4th of July Story*. New York: Aladdin, Imprint of Simon & Schuster, 1956.

"Fourth of July—Independence Day." History.com. Updated December 16, 2009. history.com/topics/holidays/july-4th.

Penny-Farthing Bikes

"Burroughs to Pedal History." *The Cricket*. July 18, 1981.

"Penny Farthing: Facts and Information." Primary Facts. primaryfacts.com/4785/penny-farthing-facts-and-information.

"Penny-farthing." Wikipedia. en.wikipedia.org/wiki/Penny-farthing.

"Penny-farthing History and Facts." Bicycle History. bicyclehistory.net/bicycle-history/penny-farthing.

"History." UDC Penny Farthings. udcpennyfarthing.com/history.

Red, White, and Blue Pancake Breakfast

Huss, John. "What's In A Name?" (lecture). Manchester Historical Society Annual Meeting Lecture, Manchester-By-The-Sea, Massachusetts. June 5, 2018. manchesterhistoricalmuseum.org/whats-in-a-name.

Huss, John. "1775—Manchester Answers the Call to Arms!" (lecture). Essex Country Sons of the American Revolution, Manchester-By-The-Sea, Massachusetts. September 29, 2018. manchesterhistoricalmuseum.org/1775-manchester-answers-the-call-to-arms.

Uncle Sam

Wiser, Kathy. "The Origin of Uncle Sam." Legends of America. Updated May 2017. legendsofamerica.com/ah-unclesam.

Bell, Danna. "Uncle Sam: American Symbol, American Icon." Library of Congress. July 1, 2014. blogs.loc.gov/teachers/2014/07/uncle-sam-american-symbol-american-icon.

Yankee Doodle

"The Origins of Yankee Doodle." The Gilder Lehrman Institute of American History. gilderlehrman.org/sites/default/files/inline-pdfs/Origins%20of%20Yankee%20Doodle.pdf.

"Yankee Doodle: Historical Period: The American Revolution, 1763-1783." Library of Congress. loc.gov/teachers/lyrical/songs/yankee_doodle.html.

Waters, Michael. "The Macaroni in 'Yankee Doodle' Is Not What You Think." Atlasobscura.com. August 24, 2016. atlasobscura.com/articles/the-macaroni-in-yankee-doodle-is-not-what-you-think.

"Yankee Doodle." Beth's Notes. bethsnotesplus.com/wp-content/uploads/2013/02/Yankee-Doodle.png.

Acknowledgements

Thank you to the staff of Manchester Historical Museum, Manchester-By-The-Sea, Massachusetts. Thank you to Susan Parker, president, and Beth Welin, director, for their wonderful suggestions and enthusiastic support of this book. Thank you to John Huss, house interpreter at the museum, for his invaluable research in his lecture "What's In A Name?" Thanks to Chris Virden, chief archivist, who uncovered a treasure trove of valuable and fascinating information of the long history of the Fourth of July parade and festivities dating back to 1829.

Special thanks to my writing buddy of many years, Mary Sue Wonson, for her unwavering support and encouragement. Thanks to Delphine Kwaa, Mia Doxee, Louise Hector, Clara Quigley, Fionna Long, and Mae Hector. Thanks to my grandchildren, Nate and Anna Gardner and Henry Collmer, for their modeling expertise and endless positive energy. Thank you to my friends Carol McKenna, Lorraine Cooper, and my twin sister Dean Donnelly. Thank you to my family: Sarah and Mike Collmer, and Andy and Allison Gardner for their generous support and interest. To my husband, David, thank you for taking these book journeys with me!

Thank you to Rebecca and Josh de Vries of the Scarlett Letter Press for their creative printing abilities and scanning skills.

This book would not be possible without the careful and expert skills and encouragement of my editor, Damaris Curran Herlihy of Curran Press, and the amazing creative skills of my designer, Cathy Kelley. Thank you!

About the Author and Illustrator

Alice has always been enchanted by festivals, fairs, parades, and celebrations of all kinds! She has especially enjoyed the old-fashioned Fourth of July parade and festivities in Manchester-By-The-Sea, Massachusetts. She has been taking photographs of the parade and festivities for over ten years. This book is a culmination of art work based on those photographs. She hopes you enjoy reading the book as much as she enjoyed creating it!